Timeline
The Journey

Anthony Vigorito

Timeline - The Journey © 2021 by Anthony Vigorito
All rights reserved. Printed in the United States of America. No part of this book may be used or reproduced in any manner whatsoever without written permission except in the case of brief quotations embodied in critical articles or reviews.

1st ed.

Cover design by Andrew Gardner

ISBN-10
ISBN-13: 978-0-9914546-3-1

1. Vigorito, Anthony, 1948- 2. Poetry

Dedication

I dedicate this chapbook to our People, heathens, savages, slaves, immigrants, outcasts, migrants, asylum seekers, and the disenfranchised that have fled and are fleeing all over the world.

May the net of the Fisherman and Fisherwoman be cast wide to encircle you all in the spirit, truth, and sanctity of the Beatitudes, with the fervent wish that you arrive safely and find the home you and your loved ones so desperately seek here in America.

About this book

Timeline marks my fifth collection.
Timeline is a medley of sixty-four poems, presenting crucial events in our country's history.

A timeline is defined as a linear graph depicting events in the order they occur, giving the observer a frame of reference. From delineating the ages of the earth, to mapping the history of any given event, a timeline reveals and truncates the much longer story.

Mysterious beginnings, man's creation of god and religion, the impact of 1619, the genocide of Native Americans, the Civil War, Industrial Revolution, coal mining, immigrant masses coming to America at the turn of the twentieth century, the Holocaust, World War II, A-Bomb, post atomic era, television, civil rights, sci-fi, sports, music of the times, crime, organized labor, and guns. The horror of addiction, the unspeakable tragedy of 9/11, Katrina, fatally flawed Middle East policies resulting in millions of Arab deaths. Ending with a plea for acceptance and forgiveness, guided by the spiritual power of knowledge, poetry, blues, science, and jazz.

There are ten "line of work" poems, a collection within the collection if you will, focusing on jobs immigrants were able to secure upon arriving here. I draw from family experience in several instances.

Please join me as I match poems to times, condensed into pivotal historical events, my America, in "Timeline."

Acknowledgements

I would like to thank my wife Ann, for her invaluable input on many levels, as well as all of the poets who have supported me and have been a source of inspiration from the beginning.
Thank you all.

I would also like to thank Andrew Gardner, photographer, desktop publisher, and friend. We have been working together since 2010, beginning with Pier 48 South Brooklyn. Our partnership has been a blessing.

Tribes	1
Mortal Sin	2
Amazing Grace	3
Wound Dresser	4
Homeland Security	5
Slaves Lament	6
Dupree's Pistol	7
Newport	8
Page One	9
Bee Loud Glade	10
Idiom	11
Line of Work I	12
Line of Work II	14
Line of Work III	16
Freedom Fighters	17
#152	18
Mission Fission	20
Lingua Obscura	21
April 15, 1944	22
Collateral Damage	23
And Baby Makes Three	24
Line of Work IV	25
Line of Work V	27
Line of Work VI	28
Farnsworth	31
Cupie (We don't stock black dolls)	33
Sister Mary Martin	34
Jetsons	35
Nonpareil	37
50 Serendipity	38
Hey Commish	39
Of All Time	40
Shoe's On The Other Foot	41
Retroactive	42
I Hope They Would Say That Ofey Is Okay	43
Fairgrounds	45

Sweet Science	46
Different	47
Whatnottoo	49
Duet (Armstrong and Teagarden)	50
Father B	51
Girl Groups	52
Line of Work VII	53
Montreaux	54
Still Howling	55
James on the Street, With a Dash of Allen	57
Drive-By	58
Grandma's Boy	59
Line of Work VIII	60
Line of Work IX	61
Etheridge and Alleluia	62
Get Well Soon	63
H	64
Bad News	65
1351	66
City Sheet	67
Funhouse Mirrors	68
Billie's Lament	69
Line of Work X	70
Fuse	71
Knee Trouble or Django the NFL	74
Gaslight (Ode to Cornelia St. Cafe)	75
Jazz Heals	76

Tribes

Lots cast in an umbral hinterland
Kismet, odds, chromosome pairs
Luck of the draw, divine providence,
Zodiac signs, astral alignment,
Proteins in the coma, intelligent design

Ancient philosophical exercise to surmise
How did we here come?
Living in the city of shadows,
Or the City of the Sun

Mortal Sin

The people have been getting nothing but bad "intel"
From religions, governments,
Psychotic families, and partisan puppets

Since the beginning of time
The word of god came word of man's mouth
From behind a screen, before movable type

Where sacramentally obscured eunuchoid pundits sat in judgment
Giving penance to sinners for their pittance
Donned in splendid vestments of silk, satin, and gold
From disenfranchised heathens over the hill
Spun Constantine's take into the greatest truth ever told

Gospels based on actionable intelligence?
Recollected one hundred or more years after his death
Casting the Gnostics aside
Deified the radical rabbi
Matthew, Mark, Luke, and John
Making a man-god of their own
An army led by the son of god is invincible

Amazing Grace

>Praise to you John Newton
>Slave ship captain who,
>In 1740 wrote a most beautiful hymn
>
>After a mid-ocean epiphany
>Heard the voice of God condemn slavery
>Left the bridge
>Abandoned the helm
>Resigned his commission
>Became a minister
>Never to transport God's first chosen children again

Wound Dresser

Neolithic shaman, prehistoric women, painted the first depictions
Dyes, charcoal, berries, blood, pigment on stone
Much later, oils on board and canvas,
Daguerreotypes, box camera photography
Motion pictures, real time war zone video coverage
The evil nature of man
The horrific face of war

Camouflaged so we won't see the bloody stump, denuded bone
The disfigured face, the amputated heart
Flag draped coffins forbidden to be photographed

The brutal hideous face of war
The unacceptable made acceptable by high righteous religious men
Compel them to undo the clotted gauze, remove the roasted skin,
Wash off brain matter, scab, and blood,
Set their broken bones and dress their gaping wounds

Then ease their bloody heads onto a clean soft pillow,
Close their bloodshot eyes, sparing them the sight
The reality of their shattered lives, and then peacefully to die
Unmask the horrors of war, see it as it truly is

Homeland Security

A concept alien to Native Americans
Neither word embraced by African slaves, nor their descendants
Terrorized for centuries by colonial invaders

As they waited with grim certainty
For another terrorist reprisal of horrific proportion
Perpetrated in perpetuity by the government,
The Klan, and the U.S. Calvary
They could count on murderous betrayal

Most think 9/11 was the first terrorist attack
Wrought from without on innocent American citizenry

Light skinned politically correct
Selective historians
European in origin

Unable to look back at so many horrors
Incapable of admitting some sought to take it all
Falsely calling it their own, in total denial,
Indifferent to human suffering, the cost, genocide

It took an enemy from without, bent on our total destruction,
To see us as one

Slaves Lament

(Cadence of O Captain, My Captain by Walt Whitman)

Father Abraham, Father Abraham
Our trip has just begun
White devil shot you in your head
Has stolen what we won

The coast unclear,
The bells we hear,
Not of us exalting,
Rather deaths toll loud o'er the land
Muting hope triumphant

Staunch the blood, hold his head
Jesus Lord, our Father Abraham
Lays there so cold, so white, so dead
Will it die with you? Will it die with you?
Is she tethered? Will she drift away?
Are we free, Father Abraham?
Papa Abraham can we stay?

Lord, help us to accept this
Oh dear Jesus hear our plea
What other white man gonna do what he did
Up and set us free

Thankfully a voice did hear
A resounding bombast that quelled their fear
There is a clearing, not far from here
Don't replace faith with doubt
Hope with fear

Look, she's up at full gallop
Winds of change brace her mane
Nostrils flared, she champs the bit
"Union" is her name

Dupree's Pistol

Trouble'll stoop you over
Buckle you way down low
Like a wispy reed blowin'
In a July delta storm

Frettin' can't bend no more Lord
Sure enough gonna break
Angry tempest brewin'
Brace me for family's sake

Achin' back creakin'
Like a rusty barnyard hinge
Trouble's stoopin' me over
Soon I fear I'll be dead

When I snatched Dupree's silver pistol
I was sober as a judge
Had no choice at that point
Knew I was good as done
Weren't nothin' on the horizon
Nothin' visible to me
Shot that white man point blank
So me and Annie could eat

They said we was worth somethin'
When they upped and set us free
Damn, we built their ivory tower
They gave us penitentiary

Calaboose wagon serpentines slow
Up that long dusty county road
Fallow gray fields, a million slave souls

Cotton fields for a jailhouse bunk
Yonder, way short of the crossroads of freedom,
Out by Highway 61

Newport

It was news to me,
They were referred to as cottages by the "captains of industry"
Fifty room stone block seaside mansions
On the soft Rhode Island shore
Visited perhaps but five weekends a year
Full staff of fifty maintained,
In case the master's work schedule changed

A cottage to the poor
Shack with an outhouse in back
The last one had better fill the bucket
Too poor to paint, too proud to whitewash
Crescent moon door
Cut with an old busted tooth saw
Bucket of water, hand pumped, drawn
From the well dug by his father
Who proudly served and was killed in the war

Centuries of free labor built the world's greatest economy
But they could care less
From atop those soft Rhode Island hills
About the generations of slaves
When cotton was king

Page One

His story, never Her story, or the fallen
Cock sure victors, bone weary vicars
Throne vagina-less homes wreaking atomic testosterone

Cruel scribed on vellum lied, justified veal on silver plates
Browned in an antebellum kitchen, or a Jim Crow café
Where Langston was told to wait
Mia culpa seldom tolls in cathedral city

Hooverville bread lines still wind past the federal vault of plunder
Where the archangels of the blues dole teller wages then foreclose

Nothing changes, spun like new silk
From the same worm's ass on snake oil TV
In good god almighty white Jesus sunshine,
On any chosen righteous Christian morning
Beams counter the path far from redemption,
Since they forgot Christ was a Jew

Sees holy Joe thump his pious pulpit,
Passing the plate for pedophile sex junkets
Trying to close conquest's gash
Still gushing through band-aid solutions
Passed late on the streets of shadows

From the scale-less congress of sorrow to South Dakota
Found gold killed them all,
Chiseled a mountain top bleached savage bones

Beneath four thumbed stone noses,
And chief Seattle's rotting bonnet
Native ghosts banshee genocides denial underfoot
Never to be read in America's history books

Bee Loud Glade, Impending Collapse of the Colony

The drone - like buzz of the bees by the hive
Was drowned out at dawn by the advent of machinery
They still keep busy in tighter quarters, they have no choice

Under a head of juggernaut boilered steam
Tooled, machined, parts, pistons, pulleys, wide leather belts,
Iron gears, sprockets, cams on shafts spun relentless in cycles,
Phases, sequences, and shifts
Days, nights, years, non - stop
As they stoked up the furnace toward progress

Fuel driven, contrived, manufactured rhythms
Whirring, whizzing, chugging, ringing
Muted earth's natural pulse, hardly heard since

As if it doesn't exist, we don't even flinch, we're so used to it
Internalized, sleep undisturbed, taken in stride
We don't even hear the din
Paying it no mind

Denying that man is fucking it all up
Finally stopping on that day
When the bees don't buzz

Idiom

Immigrants are never lessened or diminished
By their rough hewed lingo in broken English

Like a poorly tailored suit, their crudely fashioned words barely fit
With fractured parlance they struggle valiantly to be understood

Grandiose ethnic gestures help fill in the gaps
Easily shrink with embarrassment
Or beam with accomplishment when they make their point

Understandably their frustration bloats,
When a so-called native barks
"Whudja just get off the boat?"

The language of immigrants is the language of hope
Accents, dialects, provincial tongues
Should remind us of our origins, from where we did come

For it wasn't too long ago our ancestors desperately tried to fit
Coming from all over the world to America
First speaking in broken English

Line of Work I – Ode to Coal, 49 Cents a Day and Lewis Hine's Photo, "Breaker Boys"

Formed from organic decomposition,
You built the modern world,
The Hopis burned you 800 years ago
You gave us immigrants work for hundreds of years

Most lived, few thrived,
Workers barely survived the pit, the bosses, and the store
Made a meager living and died young for you on that killing floor
Working in conditions, under circumstances so grim,
American immigrant children

Till today our people, our great people live and die for you
Rock of ages, I wouldn't be here if not for you
It's where it all started back in 1905,
Three generations from that Pennsylvania coal mine

Hoodwinked, deceived, shanghai'd
Sign here Dago, now you're mine

Antonio sat in a huge coal dust covered building called a "breaker". So dark and dust filled, he could hardly see, barely breathe. There he dreamt of Erminia in Brooklyn, and when and if he'd get back to her.

In a wooden cubicle three foot square, in heavy black clothing, hat and gloves, he sat stomping chunks of coal that passed beneath him, twelve hours a day, six days a week, boys eight to eighteen, their destiny set in stone, and black lung.

He'd pick out quartz and other unwanted stones. He kept special pieces of that crystal in his coat, the breast pocket for good luck next to his heart. White, clear, cleaved surfaces, as close to a diamond he would get he thought, it would make a beautiful token of his love for his Erminia.

Forty nine cents a day, four cents an hour, they lived like that for four years (he and his brother Nicolo), saving money and making it back to Brooklyn to his beloved Erminia. Not many escaped from those merciless pits. How they got there, and how they got out I'll never know

Line of Work II - Dressmaker

Haute couture, at the top of the stairs
The bedroom in her semi - detached modest home in Brooklyn
Headless, Venus Di Milo - like breasted torso,
Padded dress form, wire cage bottom, nob - necked top
Iron wheeled figure, framed and silhouetted
By a wide bay window, next to a pedal driven
Singer sewing machine.

Swatches, snips, strips, scraps, issues strewn
Creative, frenetic scene, chairs, tables, floors, Vogue magazines.
Dressing screens, needles, fabrics, spools, patterns, scissors,
Thimbles, tufted red velvet Asian pin cushions
Waxy tapered chalk, red and white,
Mark a sleeve, a cuff, in seam, let it out, take it in,
Where a hemline's pinned
Alter again, the ever changing skirt's length,
Respect always paid to the measure of modesty
That risque joint, the stark nude knee

Sketches cut out, pictures taped to mirrors
Many pinned on those padded figures
To refer to, create anew, fit, maybe recreate
A variation on a well known theme,
To claim as her own, realize her dream
The humble creator, always kneeling
Before the standing queen's creation in the making

Down in a crouch, between her matron, the mirror, and the couch
Tape measure about, her neck craning up
Several pins tucked in the corner of her mouth.

Uptown divas pulled up in sleek black limousines
Materialized powerful women coming to Brooklyn to get fitted
In her "no - name" twelve by fifteen bedroom studio

Parading in under things, slips, brassieres, panties, stockings
Forbidden glimpses to a young boy

Came to her by "word of mouth", to purchase
Wedding gowns, dresses, pantsuits, ensembles,
As good as any from "Fashion Avenue", at a fraction of the cost
The price an immigrant visa brought
 Days long gone of high fashion and art,
In Emily's bedroom designing "salon"

Line of Work III - Kiwi

The only thing I know about my mother's maternal grandfather was that he was a master at his craft. He was key in applying the finishing touches to any well heeled man's look. His art praised mostly by businessmen on their way to or from the Court Street station on the BMT line down in South Brooklyn.

Always in a New York hurry, they'd hop up into one of the ten chairs that lined the white tile wall at the south end of the platform. Grab a paper left behind between the cushion and the frame, put one foot up at a time on the irons, as Domenic the Bootblack went to work.

Quick pass with a brush to clean, then he'd use a smaller brush to apply the polish in small tight circles with black, brown, or cream. Then he'd snap that rag and start to buff, back and forth twenty times, with intermittent snaps keeping time like a drummer. Scuffs disappeared from the speed of his buff. Five minutes for a dime, an immigrant's pay scale from another time.

Spit shine sometime, if the customer permitted.
A nasty additive to heighten the luster,
The secret ingredient of the Court Street Buffer

He'd end with a muscular snap then ask the chap to look down,
He'd say, "Dom, you're the best"
 As he could see the shine had passed the test
A shine so high it was like looking in a mirror he said

Freedom Fighters

When frightful racist backlash winds
Swept over the land like a pox, they murdered them first,

The Jews
The Journalists
The Poets
The Teachers
The Colored
The Critics
The Gypsies
The Unorthodox
The Queers
The Immigrants
The Cynics

Dread muffled public bombast, stifled dialogue and opinion
Like a brutish hand over a gasping mouth desperately trying
to deliver

Questions were deemed heresy
Surviving wordsmiths were forced deep underground to raise them
Teeming streets went hush, waiting for the tyrant to die

Candles remained lit in smoke-filled cafés down in the village
Where defiance of regime convened in dark corners
Plotting freedom in a more pure form, until the climate changed

#152

    As she polished her ornate silver Menorah,
    Seated on her porch swing in late autumn
    She noticed Joey, the neighborhood Shabbos goy open the door,
    Turn on the lights for Mr. Lieberman and his wife Molly

    Joyously anticipating the arrival of her family
    To celebrate the first night
    Deborah recalled war-torn London
    Where she had arrived safely many years before

    One of ten thousand, precious tender on the "Kinder Transport "
    As they tied her number around her neck
    That left Vienna using vigilance, stealth
    In the face of mounting humiliation and unspeakable terror

    She recollected the concern and love of total strangers
    As they spirited her away after "Kristallnacht" shattered her world
    From those she loved most, never to see them again

    Night's long shroud, pin hole pierced by a scintilla of light
    ominously approaching revealed a smiling English woman's face
    Comforting, consoling

    Thankful ghastly consequences possibly wrought
    For the risks they took,
    By a roving Nazi squad if they had been caught,
    Did not come to fruition

    She nods to herself, she understands
    How honesty's true light can be captured and bent
    By lies crushing gravity, so viciously sent

Quiet wisdom gained through grim experience
So evident in her demeanor as she ponders lessons learned hard
Looking at her menorah she began to cry
Many reasons to be thankful
Accepting where her life journey had brought her

Eight reasons to rejoice, at least as many as lights on the Menorah
The gift of gratitude afforded her a full vibrant octave of life
As Deborah recalls, and celebrates
The "Festival of Lights"

Mission Fission

He said he would rather walk through hell than send the letter
"Some recent work by", he mentioned Fermi, Joliot, and Szilard,
"leads us to believe vast amounts of energy can be released from
an atomic chain reaction with the element uranium at its core", he
stated in his earth shattering letter to FDR

Canada and the Congo have high-grade uranium producing mines,
He suggested that the US quickly secure a high grade supply

This new discovery, he goes on, will lead to the development of
most cataclysmic bombs, capable of delivering wide devastation

The race was on to be the first, hence the Manhattan Project,
under the hallowed halls of the University of Chicago commenced
its work

That letter, from the scientist to the leader,
Is I believe the reason we are living the way we are

Vast knowledge and a voice of reason,
With their collective science backing him up
Compelled our President to comply at once.
The messenger was heard and his message heeded.

Lingua Obscura

Most grave genocide
Pox infested blankets, rigor of the first biological war
Some survived, hardly thrived on government land, dirt poor

Secret coded messages, being sent and received
During times of war, necessary to deceive
A slip of the tongue brings a nation to its knees

The lost language, Assiniboine
Passed on by word of mouth,
No primers, no readers, no printed books
Its existence known by very few
Most primitive, most native of all American tongues
Proved to be their nemesis, crack proof code
Comanche, Cherokee, Choctaw, and Cree

Meskwaki, Navajo, and Seminole, all spoke code
With ironic impenetrable eloquence
And despite what this nation has done
Standing in pools of their blood
The code talkers talked under the gun

They served, and served proud despite their brutal losses
Most American among us, the only true ones belonging

The code talkers enabled us to get the edge and win the war

Then to be spoken to by the big white man in office
Referring to a sitting senator, as their princess Pocahontas
Was the height of heartbreaking disrespect
It was the final insult, "The End Of The Trail"

April 15, 1944

That black and white
Wartime wedding shot

She, in a hand sewn gown her mother-in-law made
He in his fitted army uniform, both with scared newlywed smiles

Handsome, beautiful, fit
Three stripes of rank
Framed a rainy day in Brooklyn almost seventy five years back

Stands on a mahogany stack table they received as a wedding gift
Under the letter on the wall from Harry Truman,
Commending him for his years of service
And his dog tags and discharge papers remain on the windowsill

Five years of artillery fire,
From guns that could shoot over the horizon
His ears constantly ringing, as he drums his arthritic fingers
On the arm of that favorite leather chair down in the hole

Sometimes lost, sitting long then asking,
If that photo of him and my mother is still there

Yes, I reply
As the old soldier's eyes full of sleep, close

Collateral Damage

As she waited for the Sumitomo branch to open,
To make her weekly deposit
Down on Main Street
Before school let out
Getting things done
Having to pick up her son

As that bird of prey, silent speck so high
Bombardier's crosshairs in a Norton sight zeroed in

Pamphlets ignored they said
Never realizing what Oppenheimer said he had become
The power of the sun

As Hirohito governed in denial
In that last minute, last heartbeat, last instant
One hundred thousand ghosts

Flinched at the blinding flash, facing the hypocenter, tried to cover her eyes, mid-thought, mid-breath, mid-blink, mid-sigh,

Waiting for the Sumitomo branch to open, died
Leaving a dark outline on those steps most grim silhouette,
Scorched torso of war fused into stone

And it came to pass, the aftermath as that deadly dust cleared
Some had gone insane, the crew of the Enola Gay, Tibbitts and his crew for what they had done, the orders they followed

Having to get things done, going to pick up her son
As she waited for the Sumitomo branch to open

And Baby Makes Three

I survived the flash, the blast, the mushroom cloud by chance
Coming to under the oval mahogany coffee table
With a marbleized glass top my father made
Dizzy's salty peanuts in a scalloped post-war cobalt dish,
Teetering as I reached up

Watching Million Dollar Movie on channel nine all week
Hiding the bruises the sisters of St. Joseph raised
Only to be eaten alive by mother
Sitting on her soldier's lap after the war
Smoking hot about the choice she made with crossed nylon legs
Chasing me around the dining room table 'cause I spilled my nuts
Waving grandma's spoon screaming
"Wait till you father gets home, and sees the handkerchief "

Trying to catch me and stuff me back, denying I ever happened
Wanting to start all over again
As Julia's regret tree ripened
Never bearing anything that resembled fruit, rather pits

She fumed the rooms with second hand smoke flaming blame
Only to choke when she spoke of her father
And how gentle a soul as he,
Could have upped and left her with him and me.
If only he was alive he might prevent daddy's smite,
He'd make it right

So there she was stuck with us,
A funny ungainly kid with big feet and ears
And a husband whom we feared with liquor breath and cigarettes
In the atomic shadow of his father, mirror makers in the dark
With his toxic alchemy declared bankruptcy
Down on Douglass Street in south Brooklyn

Line of Work IV - Process

In the "silver room", after huge sheets of glass known as "lights" had been removed from crates marked PPG, were then lifted and placed into a grooved dolly with ball bearing wheels at either end

The "lights" were wheeled to the cutting table, cut to size, seamed (grinding the scalpel sharp edges smooth, hand held on the spinning stone), then placed flat on a huge steam table constructed of long planks standing on edge six inches apart. Steam pipes ran the length under the table providing the wet heat of one hundred and forty degrees. The huge lights were washed, then using wooden wedges to level the surface of the glass, the water wouldn't runoff, but stand magically a half-inch high above the surface. When the glass was level, the water was removed, the application of three chemicals began.

Three ten gallon glass jars high above the table on a shelf, a hose from each jar went into a hand held "gun", with three channels. When the trigger was pulled three chemical streams met as one. Applied till the glass was covered, magically standing one half inch above the surface.

The chemicals prepare the glass for the next part of the process. Drying, then painting. silver nitrate, copper sulfate, nitric acid, carborundum, mercury, and ammonia, some of the toxic and highly dangerous chemicals used in the process.

After the chemicals were squeegeed off, and the glass was totally dry, the first coat of paint containing copper sulfate, orange in color was applied. When dry, the second coat gray in color was applied and permitted to dry. The mirror was ready to be adorned.

Thirty-six inch diameter, belt driven, wet, smooth grinding stone spinning, reservoir on top, whittled stick spout angled down Gravity pulling, water trickling, running, dripping onto the "wheel"

Old man, in a homemade Yarmulke - like skullcap
Glasses tilted forward, sitting way down on the tip of his nose
Pipe dangling from the side of his mouth, always out
Rope fastened, thick rug apron around his girth
On a wooden stool, hands guiding, thick calloused fingers,
Tips gripping mirrors he was putting the finishing touches on.

No templates, patterns, or guides
Everything done by "eye"
Pressure applied,
Height of the water coming up the side of the glass off the stone,
Determined the width, depth of the seam,
Bead, or bevel, ground and honed
Beautiful scenes etched, trellises with vines and roses,
shadow box borders, Venetian gondolas, Asian pagodas
Rendered masterfully,
Drawn on glass by eye with stone,
Dying art plied by the master, Antonio
All processes described are now done by machine,
robotics, automation

Douglass Mirror Works (On Douglass St, nr. Corner of
Henry), Antonio (Grandpa), Nicholas (Dad), Mirror Men,
John (Uncle) Sales and Installations, Joe Mirabella (The Driver),
Joe Esposito (Little Joe, Jack of all Trades), and Mr. William
Walker, (Bookkeeper)

Line of Work V - Sugar and Water (Azucar y Agua)

The Puerto Rican "Piraguero" on Douglass Street
Like the "Raspao" from Panama
Shave and flavor ice in loud shirts
In South Brooklyn and the tropics

From a brightly painted canopied pushcart
His transistor radio sings
Spoked chrome wheels on tough dry streets
He rings his bell, on the corner of Sackett and Smith
And under the fronds of the royal palms

Twelve bottles of syrupy nectar,
Plus a hidden bottle of Rum
With plastic red pourers
Rainbowed the fringe of his prized icebox
Tantalizing children with lollipop eyes
As they watch Luis scoop,
Then paper cone his icy delights

Line of Work VI - (Crime)

We're the Brooklyn kids from "up the hill"
Where the park and cemetery fix borders
Between Minerva and Lookout Hill

Whose fathers had to go on the "lam"
Whose fathers "had to go", got into a bad jam
And there was nothing they could do about it, the old lady said

Our people worked on the docks as "checkers", and "scalers",
At the car barn, fixing trolleys,
In butcher shops serving choice cuts
Driving silent electric trucks,
For the Pilgrim Laundry on Prospect Avenue by day
While some talented enough chose to fight
At the armory for Al Torre
To pad their "longie" pay, by night

We're the kids whose old men
Took federal raps for their best friends
Doing big time, for crimes back in the sixties

As grandchildren of the Brooklyn docks,
We learned to be seen and not heard,
Know our place, show respect,
And to keep our fucking mouths shut or else

Whose rascal father in one jackpot after another,
Sent Bobby to his Aunt's place,
Said it would be three days,
Then leaving them at the home on Boerum Place,
Where scary bluish meatballs and limp spaghetti
Was the "blue plate special" every Tuesday night
They did four months, thank God for aunts and uncles
And never saw him again

Who learned about tough,
In street, through attitude, manner, fear, and deed
"Tough as nails", they survived swimming in the Gowanus Canal
Came out wearing an oil, gas, paint, garbage, bloodpiss coat, feeling refreshed

We grew up with the "vig", my end, my cut, my kick, my take
Two points by Friday, payday, you better not be late

Our uncles had "crews", with shiny shoes
Who knew nothing about sailing

"Swag" was a way of life for us kids
We played with swag, we wore swag, we rode in swag,
We watched on swag, we listened on swag
If you got it swag, you scored

When the "Bust Out King" busted out the "Jewelry Emporium",
He had bought from "Al Di La"
Two years before on Eighty Sixth Street
It was a veritable "Bling-A-Rama",
All us kids got rich, ID bracelets, watches, and sapphire rings

We're the kids whose fathers sold it
And their sons and daughters died on it
Some saw our mothers backhanded
With liquor and cigarette breath, we begged them to stop

No bank accounts in their names, no checking,
No savings, only hiding places
WDPN, we don't pay no one, is where we come from

Fathers never blinked,
Came home when it was done, had a family feast

Mothers did it all, saw it all, heard it all, lost it all, survived the fall
And after all, wouldn't have had it any other way.
They had no-show jobs, led double lives, triple lives,
Perfecta lives, alive in the double lives

Speeding to the track after getting a "tip",
From Larry "Breath" Mintz on Camden Lynn,
That the Delaware "juice men" had come in
We're the kids of that "bookie", who got hurt by that six hundred dollar winner

Lessons seldom learned, some fathers are still "away".
Endless, boring, dangerous days

Remembering the story of Jimmy and Tony,
Paisanos buying a little slice of Salerno, up in Goshen
To keep the kids off the streets
And the time Johnny was driving the tractor,
With Frankie standing on the axle
Waving to us little kids from a different time
Long before the shit storm, and all the drama unfolded
Before they got in trouble,
Those tough kids from up the hill, our Fathers, our Mothers

Farnsworth

There was "Farmer Gray" cartoons on Channel Thirteen
With "Uncle Fred" doing his "Ronzoni" thing
"Ding - Dong School" with "Miss Frances"
Ray Heatherton was the "Merry Mailman"
We "Learned to Draw" with Jon Nagy
Blacks, Whites, and Grays seemed like colors to me
Put a plastic sheet right on the screen
"Winky-Dink and Me" with Jack Barry

Marionette string puppets
"Howdy Doody" emcee "Buffalo Bob"
"PrincessSummerFallWinterSpring"
That whirling vortex question mark
Used to scare the heck right out of me

Rocky Jones Space Rangers
"Rootie Kazootie", baseball uniformed rooting cupie
Hand puppets, "Kukla, Fran, and Ollie"
"Hello it's me", his name was Pinky Lee,
1950's predecessor to the 90s "Pee - Wee"

"Spin and Marty", "Diver Dan", "Superman"
"Able to leap tall buildings in a single bound",
 Soupy Sales, "Officer Joe"
"American Bandstand", "Rock "N" Roll"
At quarter to four, for fifteen minutes
Let's "Twist" some more

"Chiller Theater", Zacherley", very B horror movies
His mother was a gelatinous blob in a laundry basket
Zany, bizarre, not scary

Western heroes by the dozen Roy Rodgers, Wild Bill Hickok,
Rowdy Yates, Matt Dillon, wire Paladin San Francisco

The greatest invention Philo's TV
A new world was opening for us kids to see
We were the first generation to watch the "Tube" incessantly
I was five when it started for me back in '53
On Grandma Tessie's magical black and white
Pop–up Dumont TV

Cupie (We don't stock black dolls)

In an effort to quantify the corrosive effects
Of post-atomic TV, that for decades
Screened grinning, light families, home, land, security
The buttoned down white-picket-fenced
Crisply creased majority
On those other-than-correct in this society

Granted some ivy league academe the monies
To conduct a large sampled sociological study,
Investigating why little colored girls, when given the chance,
Chose to play with alabaster skinned, golden haired,
porcelain faced dolls
Rather than dark skinned ones consistently
Begging the question, why so early on something
so gravely wrong?

Mixed messages, double standards
Wavy images on the midway
Happy Playland's hall of mirrors
Dangled "Yes Ma'am", "Yes Sir", equality
Fostering a hollow belief that they had a shot

They did not, have not, do not, will not
Today, on this channel, with this president, in this time slot

The conclusion reached by this empirical study—
The university could have saved its money
After countless programs to undo what has been so
intentionally done,

Little colored girls, when given the choice,
Still prefer to play with light skinned dolls rather than dark skinned
ones

Sister Mary Martin

In her inimitable way,
Sub-machine gun repartee
Assured our class we wouldn't die
As sirens blared atop elevated subway stops in 1959

"If we get annihilated, the sooner we'll see God", she said
She was in the habit of making light
Minimizing the seriousness of situations

As if she were immune
Because of her commune
With church, St. Joseph and God

Bombarding us with tales of eternal life
Afforded little comfort to our class of fifty five
When we got under our desks
Put our heads between our legs
And prayed for deliverance from nuclear obliteration

Classroom dread
Certain we would ascend
Atomically
Cloud high
Christ-like
Before our time

Vaporized Catholic grade schoolers flying
Over the ruins of Bay Parkway in Brooklyn

Jetsons

Mushroom cloud,
"Boomer" times, atomic shroud
Signature feature design
Innovative refinement
Materialized as the need for speed
Was realized and achieved

Propellers screwed the "Greatest Generation" victory in place
As the war's quest for velocity
Forced their obsolescence

X-1, Yaeger's vapor trailed test run
Cracked the invisible barrier
As the world shrunk
To the deafening roar of a sonic boom

The fin, fixed variation on nature's theme, the magnificent wing
Stabilized, reducing drag, and resistance
As man zoomed faster than he had ever gone before

Finned speed,
Streamlined, demystified, aero-dynamicized
Familiarized, and globalized us all

Great distances shrunk
As powerful engines pushed vehicles to ponder creation
At the edge of the universe

Rockets, jets, cars,
Like Aunt Jenny's fifty nine Cadillac Brougham
Bikes, boats, toys
All employed the "Fin"

I remember "sending away"
For thumb sprung finned "Nike" missiles

Filled out a coupon mailed it to "Kelloggs",
In Battle Creek Michigan

It was everywhere
The omnipresent fin
Signaling the end of the propeller driven slow motion world
We all lived in

Nonpareil

Since 1953, when I first saw Rocky Jones Space Ranger
Firing his retro rockets effecting a burn to slow his descent
From the vast distant reaches of Outer Space
Noticing an increase in thrust as dust kicked up
When his ship got close to touching down on the landing pad
Magically his rocket landed vertically
I was an astounded junior space ranger instantaneously

That feat was achieved with stellar grace, precision, and ease
As Falcon Heavy's side boosters
Descended vertically from the heavens.
.
Each booster, independently powered was jettisoned,
Returning to Earth simultaneously, a burn to slow down.
Both landed with stellar grace, precision, and ease
To the screams of the students of science,
Awe, Clarke, and Asimov

Rocky Jones if you're listening,
Elon and his Team did what you did when I was a kid.
Watching "Manhunt in Space" sixty-three years ago.
Man, you writers were ahead of your time.

Then to see Starman in the Roadster with the Earth at his back,
Driving his Tesla on the stellar highway,
Blaring Bowie in the vacuum on the radio,
Waving as he goes bye,

Homage to Sci-Fi and SpaceX

50 Serendipity

Baseball, boxing, and TV combined after the war,
Like a Sugar Ray one - two,
Flush on Jake La Motta's jaw
Making peoples of colors' lot in life
Somewhat better than before

Muscular agents of social change enabled us to see,
Humanity, prodigious talent, grace, personality
Undeniable images for those who would see,
Comparative achievement readily

Made light America sit up, take notice, smell the coffee
And change forever for the better, hopefully

As Jackie danced down the third base line tauntingly,
To a more just home evening the score
The truth was as plain as the nose on your face
In a day game, or a twi-night double header

Either you can or you can't, a simple fact
And color ain't got a damn thing to do with that

A match made in heaven
The best union to me,
The marriage that is of Brooklyn, the Truth, Baseball,
And Grandma Tessie's, Black and White, Pop-up,
Dumont TV

Hey Commish

Take that asterisk out of the record books!
Reinstate old number nine as
The single season home run leader

Sixty one in nineteen sixty one
Truly a Herculean feat,
Thirty-four years to increase the Babe's count by one

Accomplished under great scrutiny and brutal pressure,
Without synthetic performance enhancers
Unless you consider a cold Rheingold,
And an unfiltered Camel as such

Which unfortunately was enough to take him from us
Too early in the game, killing us

Of All Time

His hands should have been registered
As lethal weapons of fast destruction
Float like a butterfly, sting like a bee, dancing master
Lightnin' speed at two seventeen.
Foolish white people bet their money.
What they got was a total EEEEclipse of the Sonny

Against all odds, and the white powers that be,
Wouldn't take the oath, then became Muhammad Ali.
"No Viet ever called me n....r, got nothin' against them people,
I ain't gonna go. I don't believe in no white man's religion".
The Nation of Islam, Elijah, and Brother "X",
Schooled him in dogma, faith, knowledge, and text.

"Well Muhammad, you seem a bit truculent," "Well Howard if
truculent means pretty, if truculent means unhittable, if truculent
means the greatest of all time, then I'm truculent"
The poet warrior would rant, taunt, rhyme, and rave,
The first rapper of the modern age
He predicted with accuracy the demise of his foe,
Nicknamed them all, called the round they would fall.
Taunted white America till they couldn't take no more,
Stood proud on moral grounds, from Smokin' Joe to
Larry Holmes.

Sadly forty thousand blows to the head they say,
Eight and ten ounce gloves couldn't protect,
Disease brought on by the onslaught, unforgiving and grim
But nothing could take that smile from him.

He's the greatest of all time, doubt if there'll be another,
The picture of him in a convertible with Bundini and his brother
And together they shout, "Rumble young man rumble......Ahhhh"

Shoe's On The Other Foot

It's one of my favorite black and white shots
Juxtaposition on a Montgomery bus
World turned upside down
After Rosa balked and refused to get up

Dr. King and Ralph Abernathy sitting up front
White man standing, strap hanging in the back of the bus
First come, first served, find your seat

Retroactive

Descendants of slaves
Deserve trillions in back pay, the way I figure
With interest compounded exponentially by the century

No home
No land
No security
Broken family
400 years, no paycheck
For services rendered

Ivory empire erected
On billions of bales and balls collected
Millions of acres cultivated
Hundreds of thousands fought in the war
Generations of white children catered to, educated
Just to name a few reasons
To justify monies so long overdue

Remit now!
No checks accepted
Cash Only

I Hope They Would Say That Ofey Is Okay

Saw them crackers rush the marchers on the Pettus Bridge
ABC cut into a Nazi documentary, live
Visual metaphor realized by millions
My seventeenth birthday, Bloody Sunday, March 7th, 1965
All I could do was write

Thought if that fat white pig did that to my mother
Beat down, dogs sicced, legs open, in the gutter,
I'd rack the slide, say a short prayer then lullaby the motherfucker,
Big talk for a small fry, all I could do was write

Christians? So sickening to see,
Ashamed to be an American
They don't represent me
Saw the hate in their twisted faces, the hate in their hearts
Wanted to ghost the honkies, but the Reverend said Not!
Four hundred years of housing, Marlboro, Louis Pink, Marcy
All I could do was write

Before you glow then spark, step off
Think of your art as vehicle, then floor your whip and book
Take your spiral, go viral
Everything you feel, think, imagine and see
Writer, journalist, observer, poet
In the mold of the reformed Jay-Z
All you can do to write

We're not all cut from the life on the street
As compelling, murderous, blingy may be

What about the pristine cap on the gurney,
When they slaughtered John F. Kennedy
Point being, write some wrongs at desk, studio and street
Don't go stackin' ones from here to eternity
Mix art, music, the spoken word,
An equation, formula, a passport if you will
Take the time, pop a rhyme, think about how good you'll feel

So when at night, with pen, pad and light
You find yourself lonely, blank, and bored
Don't hustle, don't cop, don't exploit your brothers and sisters,
Just write,

Because the rapper's pen is mightier than his sword

Fairgrounds
(in Memory of Kitty, March 13, 1964)

It was in that bar, in that storybook neighborhood by the Unisphere
Where they saw her every day, all the patrons knew her name

Thirty-eight blood curdling shrills
Hers went ignored in that grim vestibule of New York

They didn't even drop a dime
No one wanted to get involved
Confront the monster from the underside

So they waited behind slightly parted curtains
And hoped someone else would be brave enough, nobody was

Curled on the sash, cut short of her threshold, keys in hand
Alone in a city of eight million
If only she could have gotten her key in that door

Depraved indifference, criminal anonymity in a gray cold city

As they lined up in droves to take a futuristic tram
The perfect world showcased
On the other side of the monorail's tracks
Back in the sixties at the New York World's Fair

Sweet Science

When I heard Miles's "Jack Johnson"
Cued up on a "Dual" turntable with a "Shure" cartridge
He didn't come in right away,
McLaughlin's moody guitar
And Cobham's booming drums lead the way
For the first time in Jimmy's pad on East Broadway
Back in the grim seventies, it jazzed me away
In orbit where all I wanted to hear was that black argot
Spoke with scat, horn, skin, and eveythin'
Under the sun and Manhattan bridge

That made noise, haunting, screaming, sweet mute whispering
Crying a stream of note consciousness, circular breathing
From cats with nine lives heaving sharp axes honed over a lifetime
Gigging roadhouse juke joints in backwater times
When they were knee high

Dig it, when I heard "Jack Johnson", I got an inkling
Like I got from Billie, Sara, Dinah, and the Jive Bombers
Of what it must be like to be bold against a could care less world,
Screaming in a vacuum, low blowed, backhanded, backstabbed
Bruises you could feel but they can't see
Run but can't hide from the man and his machine
Reaching for somethin', courage, gumption
To stand and fight in the middle of their ring
With a fuck you grip on your part holding tight,
Taking on all comers
With a shunned woman who stayed for a while
Careening still mad as hell
To the Conn-Dempsey fight in a loud convertible,
Cross solid double white lines
Skidding and ditching to find,
Nobody's home

Different

Getting older, heavier, balding
Seemed destined to be alone
Everybody knew him as a great guy, which he was
Tommy's single brother Matty

Never married, "lost at love"
A "confirmed bachelor" who always showed up
To family functions with his best friend Buddy

"You know", they would say
"He's so good, very sensitive"
"That's why he's a little effeminate"
"Some creative sensitive people have trouble with intimacy"
"Marriage isn't for everyone"

Father died young, youngest son
Devoted to a doting mother, still living together, "overprotected"
Such a shame, handsome, personality, wry wit,
A "natty dresser", "neat as a pin"
All the women in the family jumped at the chance
To dance with him
Always looked good, deep in the groove, had all the moves

"You know why he's alone?"
Whispers, gestures, giggles
Walks with a "swishy" wiggle

But nothing was said to his face at family get-togethers
Where the "closet" was almost shut, relatively safe
Dark with denial, and a perverse form of respect

"Maybe he'll meet somebody someday"
He could never say that he did many times to them
Always the "loner", "odd man out", "fifth wheel", "outsider"
He could never say how he truly felt, he never came out
Who he loved, too dangerous to divulge

Such a tragedy they all would say, to die in such a terrible way
But few really understood and grieved with Buddy,
On that sad, sad day

Whatnottoo

Louis blew them blue notes new
Jazz is that wrong note played right
Dissonant note jammed in tight
What might sound wrong ain't
Late, night after night

Jazz is goin', and not knowin', never lost, except in the art
Just deep in the machinery of life, sound, and time,
Dissonance by design,
Jazz is the number eight laying right on its side

Allows for light, shadow, bearing, tempo, drift
Adapts to crowds, tastes, times, skin
Adjusts to situations, tides, and changing winds

It's a mirror with a different glimmer
Sometimes clean, crisp, sharp, no distortion
Sometimes troubled, sullen, great contortion

A seam that hard bops pristine
Not a scar, gash, scratch, or slit
Just a cool groove where same notes sound new

Can shimmer, whisper, boom, and cook
Will do what you want it to, will even take care of the Whatnottoo

Can't put your finger on it, don't even try
Jazz is the number eight laying proper on its side
Jazz is that wrong note always played right

Down the alley, up three flights,
Cross the street against the light
You lead we'll follow
Night after night after night

Duet (Armstrong and Teagarden)

Louis, (Louie) and Jack, (Big T) together
Still on stage, reflect with a song by Hoagy
About the onset, the creep of old age

Big "T" sings,
"I'm gonna fill my lungs with lots of air,
And blow with Mr. Louis Armstrong in his old rockin' chair"

Speaking in trumpet and trombone solos
As only they could do,
Their love and mutual respect so evident,
Harmony so true

"Old rockin' chair got me, Louie
Ole cane by my side, ain't goin' nowhere
Sittin' here dyin' grabbin' at them flies"
"Bring me some water Louie", says Big T
"You don't drink water", says Louie
Eyes buggin' with a wry smile
Well then Big T goes on,
"Bring me my gin son, or I'll tan your hide"
Louie goes on to remind T his hide had already been tanned
Then together they turn and broadly mug and pan

Father B

He played "Race" music at his prom
Guitar central, as he wailed Dem Bluz
Howlin' about sex, having no particular place to go, broken homes,
and fast cars with that slash, twang, and bang,
Johnny Staccato, from back up in the woods among the evergreens

Sang hoppin' on one foot, strumming across the stage,
He was the father of rock and roll,
That new variation was all the rage

He told us what time it was, it was time to rock
"Looked at my watch, it was half past ten,
She rolled me over, made me do it again,
Reelin' and a rockin', rollin' to the break of dawn"

He told us of his troubles, asking Maybelline,
Why can't you be true? citing
"You done started back doin' dem thangs you used to do"
Saw Nadine asking, "Nadine is that you? It seems every time
I see you, you got something else to do"

Pickin' up the phone, trying to pick up the pieces,
"Long distance information, give me Memphis Tennessee,
Please help me find the party tryin' to get in touch with me.
She could not leave a number, but I know who placed the call,
Cause my uncle took the message and he wrote it on the wall".
All over the world, they sure can tell
Who's playin' the guitar just like ringin' a bell
GO, GO, GO Johnny GO, Johnny B. Goode

Girl Groups

When them colored girls from Philly
Told me to meet them on South Street in '65
Man I wanted to go and I did, sure enough
Flat wooden spooned some smooth chocolate ice cream
In paper lidded Dixie Cups that July

Young Love, Baby Love, going steady,
Getting married, loyalty and fidelity
High fidelity, since stereo hadn't hit the scene
Saw Mom tappin' some toe
In that knotty pine kitchen on Fifth street
Marveling at the Marvelettes singing

Them girls rocked, and rocked hard in Shangri-La
Angel warned that masher to step off
Cause her boyfriend was back
To protect her honor, being away so long she was sure
Her Soldier Boy would save the day

I danced to the Orlons, hearin' that gutsy, "Come on boy",
Dreamed of a woman named Martha,
In Darlene Love jeans, Bobbi Soxx dreams
With that uptown Latina Carnivale shake,
Reassured me that I was her baby, hot in that fitted sequined dress
Spoke directly to us, standing erect in the third row
At the Fox on the corner of Flatbush and Nevins

Excited when the Exciters told him she was never gonna leave
him, always gonna love him, tell him, tell him, tell him, tell him
right now

Dreaming for that dream girl loyalty
Hoping that she'd never leave
Assuring her that I Would Love Her Tomorrow

Line of Work VII - Payday

Casting broad street crossing shadows,
Striping canyons as they crept
Red brick smokestacks loomed stories high
Blowing thick, east, along the river
Canvassed on a gray steel sky

Brash, young, blue-collar guys
Second generation, with strong sanguine ties to the "other side"
Punched that time clock religiously, as thirty years flew by

Union man, union job, union wages, union card
Union boss, union hall, union contracts, waterfront brawls

Carpenters framing, laborers pouring, floating, troweling
The concrete gang removed the Hico jacks,
Stripping plywood sheets when the floor dried
Then handed them up through duct shafts
To be used as forms for the next floor
Concrete craned up in hoppers
Received by the gang on the roof
Hand signals from the man on top to the operator
Determined where the next hopper full should drop

At three thirty on Friday the armored car arrived,
Traded for a numbered brass token
That hung on a "finish" nail on a board in the office
Small manila pay envelopes bulging with cash
Were passed through the paymaster's shanty window
Gross, deductions, net, in the bookkeeper's fountain pen hand
Intensely scanned for any smudged discrepancy
The top quickly ripped off, then blown into
So the cash could be grabbed with thumb and index finger
Counted, then pocketed where it belonged,
Properly seated, every Payday evening

Montreaux

At the piano muggin', "God damn it, I can't use it"
"Trying to make it real"

Cut in a small, smoky, Swiss club
High hair, short skirts,
White people snappin' their fingers drinking Cold Duck,
It was very real to me, compare it to anything

When Benny took to squawking
A gutsy, screaming raspy muted solo, so good,
Les was looking for his God and his money,
His sweet bee, and her honey
Between heaven and hell as Eddie yelled

America, you can't sell us that bag of goods
We ain't buying in, but sadly…

Our President has got his wall
And folks don't know just what it's for
Don't give us rhyme or reason,
Have some doubts, they call it treason
Looks like we always end up in a rut, God Damn It
They're trying to make it real compared to what da-da-da

Swiss Movement, "Compared to What",
Don Dean, Leroy Vinnegar, Eddie Harris, Benny Bailey,
Les McCann

Still Howling

Been more than sixty years since he taught us poets to palabra new
Inspired by the poet who wrote "Mexico City Blues"
Since he saw the best minds of his time,
Unwind, eaten alive, devolve
Lonely travelling on the road in America

Road posts screamed, move along 'cause it don't work here either
Expelled, disillusioned misfit students bleak of mind,
Who truly saw and dreamed wide eyed,
In johns, back alleys, bathhouses, boxcars
For the love of Greek gods or Corso it seems
On their knees, backs, and bellies, ball in the jack
Switched off left spur of the American central, click-ity clack
Seeking jazz, whack, forbidden sex and soup in the loop
Squatting on soapboxes of tinkered philosophy
Packed with lies from the beginning
Bummed on the northeast, or southwest negro corners of poverty
Damned the cement, aluminum, steel, silicone,
Oil atomic sphinx in yellow uranium cake

From Madison Avenue
To the lockdown wards of federal man-towns
That bashed their brains out, moiled their parts
Sucked dry their imaginations
Strapping them whirlygigging in frothy spasm
From fifty thousand volts of electroshock capitalism
Rammed down their throats daily on hydrogen TV

When leaping from twin towers in Rockland was relief
Finally escaping like Naomi
From lobotomy straight jackets free
Pancaking splat grim on flat-lined streets

Crying, sees self-sharpening surgical sprockets
Jerk heavy linked chains along shucking soul
Greased with workers where with all,
Driving this machinery of fear

Casting moral shadows on the nuclear boneyard of tears
To be judged by a scale-less "congress of sorrow"
This called home proceeds sadly into tomorrow

James on the Street, With a Dash of Allen

Bent on lug wrenching the works
Cogging the dynamic machinery in father's bleak night
He dwelled in the house of chaos

Wounded soul braced against a cold headwind
Light jacket, unfulfilled promise
Angel headed hipster
Hands in his pockets
Headed to some starry connection downtown

He moved beautifully disturbed
Through a fragile gait into our hearts

Mourning himself on the way, it seemed he knew
Lost to his destiny, burning, he walks by too quickly

Drive-By

Tiny bent down to pick up a shiny spent round in the playground
An "out of the blue" sedan rolled by, clipped fifteen rounds
Killed her older brother Eric standing behind her
He would have been the first to graduate, the first in the family
Instead he lay dead on the pitcher's mound too late in June

Daily rags trumpet these kinds of tragedies
Second amendment guarantees
One hundred times a day

And they say we're safe here in America
In Canada, Europe, Asia, Russia and Iran
Children don't face gunfire, see their schoolmates die,
Then run for cover

Arm the teachers, morons cry
The gun association and the gun makers
Are more important than your children's lives

Do nothing, then watch on TV
Pre-schoolers slaughtered on Wednesday just before three

Grandma's Boy

Little Anthony never goes outside after school
He's not allowed, truly doesn't want to, more the pity
He's scared in the projects,
Racial architects reserved for darkness

Mom never showed for him,
Grandma Artemisha his only salvation

After school, off the bus twenty past three,
Met curbside religiously

Institutional halls, steel doors, cinder block walls
Florescent glare, antiseptic white, day and night

With a feeble ring, the doors belch stench as they part
Fear escalates as they ascend noisily
Holding his hand so tight, for dear life

Artemisha knows too well
Death deals grim in those dimly lit stairwells
"Rock", "Crack", "H", "Tree",
It hasn't been her experience to see things change for the better

A culture of poverty
Depriving Anthony, seated incessantly, trance-like
Comforted somewhat playing the box
No physical activity, morbid obesity,
Biting his nails, shaking his knees
Can't focus in school, hyperactivity
Imaginary friends play with him, as a seething rage builds within
Needing to escape as Anthony so desperately does
But never will

Line of Work VIII - Golden Venture

She arrived down decks below
That ran aground off Rockaway's coast
Alone in a sea of humanity
Like so many of our people, one hundred years ago

Never finding streets paved with silver or gold
Rather, bottles and cans,
In the pouring rain and winter's cold
Her cherished dream scrounged
From the bottom of stinking garbage cans
At daybreaks peep, or very late, quietly closing the gate
To avoid the scorn of irate homeowners

Like an ant carrying one hundred times her weight
Aluminum mountains in clear plastic bags
Atop shopping carts with obstinate wheels
The shy redeemer saved every cent religiously

Awaiting that glorious day in the year of the rooster
When she could send for her two sons, Yanbo and Chen
Her tireless redemptive efforts
To retrieve, nurture, and educate them
When joyously they come
Becoming proud Americans

Line of Work IX - The Shape Up

They "shape up" on the southwest corner of the cemetery,
Six in the morning

Always looking for work, as passing cars honk, and trucks stop
They know from "word of mouth", skilled workers are found there

Pintadoras!, the driver of a step van yells, as he profiles the men
Si, five laborers say, siete cuadros need to be painted today
Eight bucks an hour, they said OK, and got in

Broken English speaking, skilled laborers, desperate for work
Shape up on cemetery corner, every morning

Scared, hungry and sick of trying
Wondering sometimes, Is it better here than it was down there,
Or back on the other side?

Etheridge and Alleluia

Right next door to one of those white lace curtain,
Storefront "Unification" churches off of Smith St. downtown
A plastic Jesus flashes
His neon halo attracting passers-by
As they window shop for God

Sits a happening gay bar, not run by the mob anymore thank god
When they would charge for protection, a goon guards the door,
Watered down drinks patrons couldn't afford
When somebody balked they were shown the door

Where perched patrons patronize trying their luck
Just like in any other gin mill in hook-up city

City dichotomy configured,
Parallel universes, so seemingly distant
By a crumbling partition of ignorance, a mere eight inches wide

As they come out to smoke,
In accordance with the mayor's new tobacco ordinance
Meeting and greeting the righteous in the clouds

As that wall dissolves outside respective confines
For a short while curbside, in south Brooklyn

Get Well Soon

Trip wired, beady-eyed heads shy from the light
Like deer stunned in hunter's brights

Muddying their buzz drinking wine under the Highline,
They trolled for some strange
Down by the terminal market in the rain

Strung out meat stickers, bone weary sorry hipsters,
Gripped their yanks holding dear hot for something fine,
Leery of bad trade out there, tried to behave

Addicted to getting their nut with a good lump on, came up empty
Dope sick, limp dicked, traipsed back to the rack in the park
Craving naked lunch in the dead of night they resigned to jones
When out of the blue, Flacco showed

Then just like that,
All those grim faced, flat lined,
Starving stem hoppers leaped with glee
'Cause suddenly everything got right
In Wonderland that night

H

Butaned spoons bubble rock to liquid
Hollow needle fiends from downtown narcotic city
Tied off behind the church
Booting crimson ribbons back into eyedropper viral works,
They moaned as fear and pain neutralized
Into a hooded eye warm central glow of high

They zombied in the dead of night,
Infernal land of blood, nod, and vomit
Shuffling over logoed glassine bundles they shot

Ascended a crystal stair to heaven,
Overstayed their welcome
Rousted by Mother Jones,
Tossed out on the corner of the killing floor, they froze

Glowing filters between blistered fingers,
Quaking to neither wind nor music came to
Deep in denial, with a deadly case of the "fuck its"

Squinted as the sun came up,
Thinking today might be the day to try
But sadly did the same,
Copped on limbo boulevard again

Bad News

Thankfully for most of us,
There are only a few days in our lives
Where horror, tragedy, disbelief and sorrow
Freeze frame a dark days circumstance
Stark after ten thousand tomorrows

Where you were, what you were doing,
In school, at a job,
Day, night, season, year
Tattooed indelibly, unmuddied clarity,
Year after year

TV, radio, newspapers, multimedia
Through the "grapevine" on the street
Gasps, sobs, sighs stagger the truths delivery
The unimaginable heard for the first time
The harbingers tale of woe
Denied, defied, decried

All day long a lamenting chorus of woe
"It couldn't be",
"You've got to be kidding me",
"Oh God no"
A national hoax, a misprint, a misquote
"My Father didn't come home"
"It's so hot I'm burning up",
"Stay on the line they're coming"

As doubt crumbles slow into reluctant acceptance
Under the crushing weight of the undeniable truth, it's inescapable
The most horrible, unbelievable, frightful thing has happened

1351

    Elevator, six floors, "pre-war " apartment building
    Much like the one where I was born
    That blocked that horrific view, from their corner classroom
    Overlooking a numbered side street and avenue in Brooklyn

    In the office our shattered staff had a vantage from the other side
    Burning fuel, black, thick, licked its way up the tower
    Blowing grim across the river

    Then a fine golden dust filled a sparkling morning sky
    Collecting on the roof, hood and trunk, a thin golden line
    Along the wiper blades on the windshield

    We cried, but never let on, it would never come from us
    Just like any other beautiful pre-war Brooklyn day
    At P.S. 192 that Tuesday

    Spared them, at least until the bell rang at three
    From seeing where the first, second millennium,
    Religious war began

City Sheet: Remembering the Days When Newspapers Were Read on the Subway

With no knowledge of the Asian art, Origami
Indigenous urban news scanners
Transporting on rails in tight quarters
Practiced a variation on its theme
Underground every morning

Witnessing the rookie doing battle with
"All the news that's fit to print"
One readily sees the challenge it presents
In creative paper management

With emphasis on plumb columnar folding techniques
Specific article isolation and framing

With a working knowledge of the pinched crease,
Bending ink, lap pressed pleats

One needs a degree, or soon a fool shall be

Reconfigured from page to page,
Ably maintained within the confines of a considerate space.

Funhouse Mirrors

They see us as arrogant, irreligious,
Intellectual, illegally unionized, treasonous
No borders, immigrant loving
Baby killing, n****r loving, urban dwelling miscreants
Degenerate, with a god-less bent on anything straight
From liberally compromised blue Yankee states

While we see, a sea of rightly scriptured incredulity
Fundamentally flawed Oral Roberts clones
Taking a bottle of bible as medicine
Rather than a teaspoon of science every morn
Packing a genetic pre-disposition to anti-intellectualism, exclusion,
Beer, postal violence, racial hatred and unregistered guns
Window racked in cousin Earl's old Dodge pick-up
Known for flooring it when the needle's on "E",
Twice or more removed at least
Definitely asleep at the wheel

The chasm is deep and the bridge is out
Go Fuck Yourself American Cable TV

Billie's Lament

Baby kisser assurances and promises ring hollow
Like, "You're doing a heck of a job Brownie"

Toppled steeples spear noxious mud
An eighty-seven white Chevy with tidal levels striping its doors
Tell of the rise and fall
In our soulless third world hinterland, New Orleans

Down in the ninth ward, less than before, nothing at all
Random tangle of context-less things, dashed tumble of furniture

Bodies rot on post atomic streets
Strange fruit twist on bone yard trees
Dreams decay in the slime of racist apathy

Rainbow molds blight phantom homes
Virulent spores spread a cough
All frame quarters face bulldozing
Suicides spike

As they rebuild category three walls, refuse to ask the Dutch,
For their knowledge, experience, and help
To those same unacceptable government specs
Below future levels and acceptable standards again and again

Line of Work X - Round Trip

T-car drivers, the T on the license plate means taxi, airport bound
Double park on the overpass bridge
Waiting for the dispatcher's call

Chatting over idling engines in Pashto
Through open windows on any given summer day
Probably complaining about how little they get paid,
Directional advice, maybe some of that old time religion,
Tales of the old folks, old times,
Worries brought to counsel on the expressway bridge

They cut their engines when it's really hot
Park it under a tree, hoping for a breeze
Gas around four, so they sweat it out
Under that line of Eighteenth Street sycamores

Saving money, and thinking it's not that bad here in America,
It could be worse, citing the time he dug a footing hole
In one hundred degree heat little to drink or eat,
For a mean man who shorted him
Hard labor, fifteen hours a day, under a brutal sun

Old stories, the daily dose of medicine immigrant's take
To ease the fear and pain from leaving their homeland

They remember those times,
Waiting on the Seeley Street Bridge for the dispatcher's call
Still secretly wishing they were driving home.

Fuse

Six fingers on the sidewalk
Styx riled with rigor stinks
God's pointing at each other
Mad Bombers on the streets

Holy desires
Faithless smiles
Deviant bent
Twisted wires

Impugn religion
Righteous schism deep
Leaders with no vision
Mad Bombers on the street

Sell weapons the world over
WMDs guaranteed and cheap
GIs died finding them in Bukabah and Afghanistan
Mad Bombers on the street

Asked Russia to hack US for her e-mails
They started the next day you see
Sold our agencies down the river to the Czar in Helsinki
Mad Bombers on the street

Disrespected our most revered allies
Knows more than the generals he guarantees
Fell in love with the Korean madman
Who lobotomized and murdered Otto
Mad Bombers on the streets

Threw paper towels to the victims of Maria
Tax cuts for your "fat cat" elites
Let Russia cleanse Syria
Mad Bombers on the street

A band of Saudi killers
Killed Koshoggi on world wide TV
Depraved whores for weapon money
Mad Bombers on the streets

Knows more than Nobel scientists
Global warming a left wing scheme
Must reduce carbon footprint by 80% as they privatize
Mad Bombers on the streets

Anti-American hatred of the immigrant
An Israeli-like wall is key
Immigrant children put in American made cages
Mad Bombers on the streets

They'll sacrifice fifty million
Glitch on some radar screen
Big Brother will take full responsibility
Mad Bombers on the streets

Cutthroat corporate terrorists
Leave ghost towns when they flee
Flint's got no motherfucking drinking water
Mad Bombers on the street

Said there were good people on both sides,
Like a Nazi sympathizing rebel creep
Forgot the bloody legacy of WWll, seventy million dead
Mad bombers on the street

Pulled our forces out of Syria
Created a murderous vacuum for the world to see
Abandoned our valiant Kurdish allies
Mad Bombers on the streets

Don't despair the market's up
All indicators bull
Money ghouls optimistic
As a blast levels your shithole neighborhood

Bloody men
Bloody hearts
Not a one can think
They all drink from the dead man's skull
Mad Bombers on our streets

Knee Trouble or Django the NFL

Take a stance, effect a gesture with crucial social measure
Freely speak the words forbidden to be uttered

Bellow from the street up,
Straight from your soul, heart and the gutter
Don't censor shit in any way
When they muffle our bombast the beast will reign
Give 'em plenty of lip, right from the hip

How many times have you seen a white male shot
While crossing the street, seventeen times in the back?

How many times have you seen a fourteen year old white boy
Murdered for whistling at a woman,
A heavy industrial fan tied around his neck,
Thrown off a bridge into a river?

How many times have you seen innocent white girls
Petticoats, pig tails, in their Sunday best blown to bits
While praying with their families in a Baptist church?

The QB took a knee, to peacefully protest police brutality
His intent, not in defiance of our flag,
Or our veterans who proudly serve

Rather to bring nationwide attention to brutal problems
That have plagued our people since sixteen nineteen
Still another athlete of color, blackballed for being black
Sidelined from earning at a job he prepared for all his life
Take a stance, effect a gesture with crucial social measure
Django the NFL

Gaslight (Ode to Cornelia St. Cafe)

Quiet echoed loud, that cobalt blue Monday night downtown
Haunting lanes wind time back
Bright round old neon, tired green door, rouge brick wall
Spoke of grandfather's clock rewound

Storied ghosts peeked,
Sure I saw Grandmaster Rossilimo
In his window on Thompson Street

On to the cafe, home of the salon,
Sacred place of candlelit small table, shoulder to shoulder
Worker among workers underground intimacy
Where defiance is served hot in a haze of DuMaurier,
Before the ordinance, at the dais of dissent

Folktales, folk songs, folk culture, folk music,
folklorists, folk art, passionate folk
The salon's place, coffeehouse mission

As we were warmly greeted by Robin at the foot of the stairs
A podium for poets, ears for musicians,
Stage for actors, harbor for heretics,
Church of the human condition

Where dissident candles burned bright despite the state
Keeping truths and facts alive
Down in the now gone recesses of the cafe artist salon

Jazz Heals

Idea: Jazz World Music and Poetry Day
From the Mosque at Ground Zero

As Maya reminds us,
We are more alike, than we are unalike
We are much more alike, than we are unalike my friend

Relax, dream, revel in eastern culture, its history and beauty
The influence of the east is seen, heard, and felt
At the four corners of the Earth
Know, starting with Abraham's son Ishmael, Islam was begun

Dogma, Architecture, Art, Music, Food, Dance
Whirl dervishly, arch triumphant, science, mosaics,
Lattice, inlaid, and poetry woven
In our hearts, minds, bodies and souls

Muslim musicians, African American Muslim Jazz musicians,
Who rejected the white man's god,
Like our late brother Ahmed Abdul Malik
Who got his Phd. in the implementation, use, and integration
Of traditional Islamic instrumentation
Will be our spiritual compasses

Healing is the key, as we cross to Jazz Sahara
A silent caravan carrying priceless Arab treasure
On a Kind of Blue, Night in Tunisia makes its way

With bowed heads, and a Sufi reverence for poetry, art, and music,
we proceed, truly hear the instrumentalists speak in Oudanese,
Dutenese, and Kanoonenese

Chording with Mother Africa, Israel, ancient Persia, and America,
Rahsaan blows both horns with one mouth, again summoning the
walls to collapse bringing us full circle to the oasis

Where to drink
Where to ease
Where to love
Where to truly be a Human Family

Pontiff Jazz musicians will ease our fear and pain
As we bridge the racist chasm
And cross the abyss to Jazz Sahara

www.ingramcontent.com/pod-product-compliance
Lightning Source LLC
Chambersburg PA
CBHW020430010526
44118CB00010B/505